Jeff Rosalsky
79 Fair Fairview Ave.
Woodcliff Lake N.J.

The Jews Helped Build America

Books by Arlene Harris Kurtis

THE JEWS HELPED BUILD AMERICA
PUERTO RICANS: From Island to Mainland

The Jews Helped Build America

by Arlene Harris Kurtis

Illustrated with photographs

 Julian Messner • New York

Published simultaneously in the United States and Canada by Julian Messner, a division of Simon & Schuster, Inc. 1 West 39 Street, New York, N.Y. 10018. All rights reserved.

Photo Credits

Amalgamated Clothing Workers of America: p. 64
Mrs. Esther Bibbins: p. 83
B'nai B'rith: p. 31 (right)
George Eastman House Collection: p. 35
Federation of Jewish Philanthropies: p. 87
Friedman-Abeles: p. 45
Goodman Matzoh Co.: p. 60
ILGWU: p. 63
Israel Govt. Tourist Office: p. 53
Jonathan B. Kurtis: p. 23, 52, 56, 57
March of Dimes: p. 74
Museum of the City of New York: p. 42
———The Byron Collection: p. 37
———The Jacob A. Riis Collection: p. 41
New York Philharmonic: p. 77
New York Public Library Picture Collection: p. 20, 29, 47
Religious News Service: p. 54, 86
Philip Rubin: p. 24
Levi Strauss & Co.: p. 31 (left)
Temple B'nai Jeshurun, New York City: p. 22, 55
Temple Beth Elohim, Charleston, S.C.: p. 27
Temple Israel, Tulsa, Oklahoma: p. 22
United Nations: p. 76
United Press International: p. 11, 13, 71
U.S. Department of the Interior: p. 16, 28
YIVO Institute for Jewish Research: p. 33, 36, 62, 68, 84
Zionist Archives: p. 67, 69, 75

Printed in the United States of America

ISBN 0-671-32313-X Cloth Trade
0-671-32314-8 MCE

Library of Congress Catalog Card No. 73-123166

DESIGNED BY LEON KOTKOFSKY

To my parents, and to Alan

ACKNOWLEDGMENTS

THE STORY OF the Jews in America is like a rich fabric with many different threads. In selecting the threads to weave into the story told here, I have had the generous guidance of many people. Among them are Lee M. Hoffman, my editor; Rabbi Gunter Hirschberg, who read the manuscript more than once and made valuable suggestions; and my dear father-in-law, Max Kuritzky, who was born in Russia in 1883, and shared with me the details of his life there and his early years in the United States.

I am also grateful to Rabbi Louis I. Newman and Elizabeth Kamenetsky of Congregation Rodeph Sholom of New York City for the use of the temple library. The Synagogue Architectural Library of the Union of American Hebrew Congregations was also most helpful.

CONTENTS

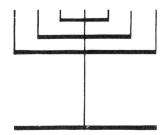

CHAPTER ONE

Why They Came

"I SEE FIRE, MOMMA," said seven-year-old Jacob.

Since early evening, there had been rioting in the small Jewish village in the Russian countryside where Jacob Markowitz and his mother lived. Now at dawn, flames from burning houses on the main street were lighting the sky.

A band of armed horsemen had ridden into town with orders from the Russian Czar to punish the Jews. Their cry was "Death to the Jews who cheat our peasants!" The peasants of nearby villages ran behind the horsemen. They turned on any Jewish shopkeepers they could find, looting and burning their stores and homes.

"Get away from the door!" cried Jacob's mother in a frightened voice. Jacob crouched down in the small darkened room behind his mother's tailor shop where they also lived. They hoped they would be overlooked by the rioters. In two days they were to start out on the journey to America to join relatives there.

This was not the first time Jacob's town or the Jews in Russia had been attacked. They had been mistreated for many years because of their religion. The Russian Orthodox Church was the official religion. But the Jews had their own religious beliefs and refused to change them.

Since the 1700s, the Russian government tried to force the Jews to change. They were denied citizenship. They were ordered to live in a district called the "pale." This was a strip of land that stretched from the Baltic Sea in the north, to the Black Sea in the south. Within that area, Jews could move around. They searched for better soil to farm or crowded into towns looking for work. But the borders of the pale were like a noose around the Jews' neck. The government kept drawing the noose tighter, as time after time they reduced the size of the pale.

Laws passed in 1880 made life even worse. Jews had to pay a double tax on money they earned. Their district was made even smaller. But most terrible of all were the riots. The cossacks, the Czar's horsemen, were sent out to attack Jewish towns.

After 1880, the Jews of Russia began to leave this hostile land. They wanted to go to the United States. There they knew they could become citizens and still remain Jews. In the United States, government and religion were separate. A person could follow any religion he chose.

In the next years, thousands of Jews left Russia and Poland for America. Life was hard for the millions who remained. In 1905, the rioting was widespread.

A troop of Russian cossacks about the year 1905.

"The cossacks are here!" was a cry of fear heard in over fifty Jewish towns. Hundreds of Jews were killed and over 40,000 shops and homes were looted.

Jacob's town was one of those attacked. As he crouched in the darkened room with his mother, he could hear the thunder of horses' hooves and the screams of terror outside.

Suddenly there was a crashing at their door. Two huge peasants strode into the room. One carried an iron rod and the other an axe.

"We come from the Czar!" roared the one with the rod. "Leave or be slaughtered!"

Jacob shivered with fear. He made a move to hold on to the top of his right boot. He wanted to protect the money and steamship tickets hidden there. But he caught his mother's fearful look, which meant, "Hold still!"

The peasants looked around to see what they could take of value before they set the house ablaze. One of them carried the sewing machine outside.

"There is nothing else worthwhile here," grumbled the other peasant, and he began breaking up the worn table and cupboard with his axe.

Jacob and his mother moved to pick up the two bundles that contained their clothes. This was all they would be able to take with them. In the center of one of the bundles, Mrs. Markowitz had hidden her precious brass candlesticks, used on Jewish holidays.

She held her breath as the man with the rod kicked at her bundle. "Rags," he grunted as he left.

Mother and son joined the streams of fleeing Jews who were hurrying to the next town. The railway station there was thick with people. They would have to sleep on the platform that night and try to squeeze aboard the train that came the following morning.

Mrs. Markowitz bought a ticket from a railroad official. She knew he charged her more than he should, but she had no choice. She had to pay what he asked. Jacob and his mother did not have official passports giving them permission to travel to a foreign country. They paid a guide to take them secretly across the border into Germany. From there, they traveled by train to Rotterdam, Holland. They had to part with more of their dwindling supply of money to pay for beds and meals at a travelers' house on the dock. There they waited for their ship, the *St. Paul,* to arrive. On the day they boarded the *St. Paul,* they had sixteen cents left. Like most immigrants, they would arrive almost penniless in America.

In 1905, passports and money were not required to enter the United States. All an immigrant needed was to prove he was healthy and had a relative who would vouch or be responsible for him. Mrs. Markowitz and Jacob had relatives who would vouch for them.

The first of their family to go to the United States had been Mr. Markowitz and his daughter Ida. They had been sent tickets by Tevye Tupinsky, the young man from their town whom Ida

Jews trudge the dirt roads to the next village, after a riot in their Polish town. Poland was part of Russia in 1905.

Would they ever see each other again? The family poses together in Russia before two of them leave for the United States. Like the links in a chain, each member sent for another, until many years later, the family was re-united in America.

planned to marry. Some years earlier, Tevye had run away from the Russian army. When he reached New York City, he had no one to vouch for him. But Tevye was trained as an ironworker, and government officials knew he could find a job right away. So Tevye was allowed to enter the United States.

As soon as Ida arrived, she and Tevye were married. They worked with Mr. Markowitz to save money to bring Mrs. Markowitz and Jacob to New York.

Many families were like this one. Each member was a link in a chain, saving to send for the next one. But soon after Mr. Markowitz arrived, he died of pneumonia. For a while the chain was broken. Ida and Tevye had to work five more years before they could send for Mrs. Markowitz and Jacob. Now at last, they were on their way.

On the *St. Paul,* their small ship, Jacob and his mother slept in bunks below deck. This area was called steerage, because the ship's steering machinery was located there. Night after night Jacob tossed in his bunk as the ship rumbled and the gears ground against each other. He heard the sounds of people being sick from the motion of the boat. Babies cried.

During the day, passengers went on deck to get away from the noise and the foul smell below. Jacob breathed the fresh air. His mother brought him a piece of dried cod fish and a boiled potato to eat on deck. It was better eating with the wind blowing at him, than sitting at the crowded tables in steerage.

Even though it was only September, it was cold at sea. Jacob saw a man who warmed himself by standing next to the smokestack on the deck. The man had had to sell his overcoat to help pay for his ticket. This was the only way he had to keep warm.

On the day they were to arrive, Jacob and his mother were up before dawn. Now they stuffed their clothing into a large potato sack Mrs. Markowitz had gotten from a crewman. They went up to the deck.

The railing of the ship was lined with other immigrants, clutching their bundles and their children. The *St. Paul* sounded its foghorn announcing its arrival in New York Bay.

The Statue of Liberty greeted all immigrants as their ships entered New York Bay.

Plaque of the Statue of Liberty with the words of a poem by the Jewish-American poet Emma Lazarus.

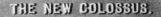

THE NEW COLOSSUS.

NOT LIKE THE BRAZEN GIANT OF GREEK FAME,
WITH CONQUERING LIMBS ASTRIDE FROM LAND TO LAND;
HERE AT OUR SEA-WASHED, SUNSET GATES SHALL STAND
A MIGHTY WOMAN WITH A TORCH, WHOSE FLAME
IS THE IMPRISONED LIGHTNING, AND HER NAME
MOTHER OF EXILES, FROM HER BEACON-HAND
GLOWS WORLD-WIDE WELCOME; HER MILD EYES COMMAND
THE AIR-BRIDGED HARBOR THAT TWIN CITIES FRAME.
"KEEP ANCIENT LANDS, YOUR STORIED POMP!"
      CRIES SHE
WITH SILENT LIPS. "GIVE ME YOUR TIRED, YOUR
      POOR,
YOUR HUDDLED MASSES YEARNING TO BREATHE FREE.
THE WRETCHED REFUSE OF YOUR TEEMING SHORE.
SEND THESE, THE HOMELESS, TEMPEST-TOST TO ME,
I LIFT MY LAMP BESIDE THE GOLDEN DOOR!"

THIS TABLET, WITH HER SONNET TO THE BARTHOLDI STATUE
OF LIBERTY ENGRAVED UPON IT, IS PLACED UPON THESE WALLS
IN LOVING MEMORY OF

EMMA LAZARUS

BORN IN NEW YORK CITY, JULY 22ᵗ 1849
DIED NOVEMBER 19ᵗᴴ, 1887.

A moment later, the Statue of Liberty, her arm outstretched, could be seen through the morning haze. A cheer went up!

People began crying and kissing each other. Jacob grinned as he felt his mother's wet cheek against his. He began to cheer along with the others.

They had made it! At last they were in the United States.

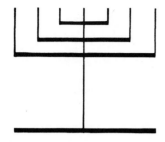

CHAPTER TWO

An Ancient Heritage

THE JEWISH RELIGION would shape Jacob's life in America, just as it had shaped the lives of Jews down through history. The places where Jews lived, the food they ate, the kind of work they did, their sense of justice, all were tied in with their religious beliefs.

The very first Jews were a group of twelve tribes called Hebrews. They lived four thousand years ago in the land of Canaan. This area, later named Palestine, is at the eastern end of the Mediterranean Sea on the continent of Asia.

About 900 B.C., some of the tribes settled in the north of Palestine and called their kingdom Israel. Israel was the name of the father whose sons were leaders of the twelve tribes. Two other tribes settled in the south, and called their kingdom Judah.

This was the name of one of the sons. Centuries later all Hebrews came to be called Jews after Judah's name. Their religion was known as Judaism.

The Jewish religion set the tribes apart from the other peoples of the lands in which they lived. Most of the ancient peoples believed in many gods. They prayed to idols in the shape of humans or animals. But the Jews believed in one God. They were the first people to work out the idea of an all-powerful unseen God.

They had their own Hebrew language and alphabet. Their first writings were on stone. Since it is easier to cut stone by moving from right to left, this is how Hebrew is written. Later, when the writing was done on sheepskin, the same system was followed. All Hebrew books today still read from right to left.

When the early sheepskin writings were rolled around two smooth shafts of wood, they were called scrolls. The scrolls contained the history and ideas of the Jews, written over a period of a thousand years. Later, these writings were put together in a book called the Holy Scriptures or Bible.

Two of the world's great religions adopted the Hebrew Bible. The Christians called the Bible the Old Testament. Then they added a New Testament of their own. The Muslim faith is also based on the Hebrew Bible.

Although Jews and Christians agreed on many ideas, there were points of difference between them. These differences came to have dreadful meaning to Jews in many parts of the world.

The Jews and Christians differed in their understanding of Jesus Christ. Most of the Jews respected Jesus who was a teacher and a Jew. Others went further. They believed Jesus was a savior or Messiah sent by God. These Jews became the first Christians. To them, Jesus was holy. But the Jews did not believe even Moses, their great teacher was holy. They could not accept Jesus as holy, or as the Messiah, and still remain Jews.

Nevertheless, Jews and Christians existed side by side for many years. Troubles between them came after A.D. 70. Then the kingdom of Judah was destroyed by the Romans. Jews began to look for homes in other countries. At first they were welcomed in Spain and France. In these lands they reached high positions and enjoyed the respect of their fellow countrymen. But Christianity was spreading throughout Europe. Rulers saw a way to unite and control their people by demanding that everyone follow one faith. All others were persecuted, including Jews.

In 1267, the Jews in Austria, who were once welcomed, were now forced to wear an ugly cap that marked them as outcasts. In Spain they were made to wear a long cloak and a badge. On the

An old sketch showing the stoning of Jews in England during the Middle Ages.

threat of death, whole towns of Jews converted to Christianity. In France in the 1300s, Jews were told to wear a red and yellow badge.

More and more the Jews of Europe kept to the safety of their own part of town, called the ghetto. Still they were blamed for troubles not of their making. The Jews became the scapegoats of history.

But despite persecution, the Jewish faith survived. And Jewish children played a vital part in this survival. For thousands of years, wherever Jews went in the world, their scrolls and Bibles went with them. The children learned from them, and then they taught the laws to their own children. So it went from one generation to another.

The Bible the children learned from contains twenty-four books. The first five are called the Books of Moses or The Torah. The Torah contains the Ten Commandments and other laws about how people should treat one another.

Since the early people who wrote the laws were farmers, many of the laws were written in the language a farmer would understand. Jews were instructed to give fair weights and measures. They were directed to leave a corner of their fields unpicked, so that a stranger, passing by, could find food. They were told to shelter the homeless.

Some of the laws had to do with daily life. Rules for cleanliness and the safe preparation of food were set down in the Torah. Fit and proper ways of living were contained in the kosher laws. "Kosher" is the Hebrew word for proper. Jews made every effort to keep "kosher" in the countries in which they lived.

The Jewish faith survived because the laws were passed down from parents to children. Youngsters conduct services at Temple B'nai Jeshurun in New York City. The boys wear skull caps (yarmulkas) and prayer shawls. The Torah scroll was taken from the ark behind the velvet curtain. The candle holder (Menorah) is a symbol of the Jewish faith. The six-pointed Star of David appears on the altar.

The Ten Commandments are cast into the walls of Temple Israel in Tulsa, Oklahoma.

The Hebrew letters look something like 7 W D. Hebrew is read from right to left, and these letters stand for k, sh, r, (kosher). This is a shop on a busy Brooklyn street.

Mrs. Markowitz had kept the kosher laws in Russia, and she would do so in America, too. Jacob would never eat dairy products and meat together, because this was forbidden by the laws. He might have a hamburger made of kosher meat, but he would never eat a cheeseburger! The reason is that cheese is a dairy product and therefore it cannot be mixed with meat.

Jacob would never eat pork or shellfish, such as shrimp, because they are forbidden by the laws. His mother would keep separate dishes, pots and utensils in the kitchen she would share with her daughter Ida. One set would be for meat meals, the other for dairy meals. She would even have separate soap and towels with which to wash and dry the dishes.

The Jews are commanded to keep one day of rest each week. "Remember the Sabbath to keep it holy," read the words of one of the Ten Commandments. The Sabbath falls on Saturday of each week. It is a day of rest and worship. No fires are permitted to be made because no work can be done on Saturday. This is a time when Jews attend a house of prayer—a synagogue or temple —where they read over the law and try to refresh their spirits.

In the temple, the Torah scroll is kept in a special case called the ark. When the Torah is to be read, it is removed from the ark. Then the fine cloth covering the scroll and the silver ornaments that decorate the tops of the wooden shafts are put to one side. The scroll is placed on a large table, and the reader rolls it

An open ark at Temple Sholom in Springfield, Ohio. The covered scrolls each have their own silver pointers. Above the ark is the eternal light, which must always be kept burning.

from one shaft on to the other. To further protect the precious parchment, the reader does not touch the words with his finger as he reads. Instead, he uses a silver pointer. It is a great honor to read from the Torah.

Temple scrolls are still carefully written by hand as they were in ancient days. When a scroll becomes too worn to be used, it is buried in a safe place.

In their homes, Jews remind themselves that they live by Torah law by putting a small metal or wooden case containing a tiny scroll on the doorpost. This scroll is called a Mezuzah, the Hebrew word for doorpost. Some people wear a silver or gold Mezuzah on a chain around their necks.

Respect for the Torah and the ancient laws of justice and charity has been a guide to Jews everywhere for thousands of years.

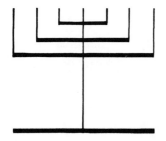

CHAPTER THREE

Where They Settled

TWO-HUNDRED AND FIFTY YEARS before Jacob's ship steamed into New York Bay, the first Jews came to America.

These settlers were originally from Spain and Portugal. In 1492, the same year in which Christopher Columbus discovered America, the Jews were forced to leave Spain. Their Catholic majesties, King Ferdinand and Queen Isabella, declared that only Catholics could live in their country. Later, Portugal made the same rule.

Some of the expelled Jews settled in Brazil. Then, in 1654, twenty-three Jewish men, women, and children from Brazil arrived in New Amsterdam, the city that would one day become New York.

These first families were followed by others. The Spanish and Portuguese Jews spread out to six of the thirteen colonies. They took an active part in the life of the new land.

Some were planters, like Francis Salvador, who settled in South Carolina. Others were traders in New England. Aaron Lopez of Newport, Rhode Island, was the owner of thirty sailing ships that carried goods between Europe and America, and the West Indies. Asser Levy, the leader of the New York Jewish community, was a butcher. A special ruling was made that excused him from selling pork in his store.

Haym Salomon was a Polish Jew who came to New York during the American Revolution. Salomon served as a spy for General George Washington. Later, as purchasing agent for the Revolutionary army, he helped supply the soldiers with clothing and guns.

In 1775, young Lieutenant Francis Salvador (center) was shot by Indians and scalped. This mural of war heroes is in the Beth Elohim Tabernacle in Charleston, South Carolina. The Temple was established in 1750.

The interior of the Touro Synagogue in Newport, Rhode Island which was built in 1763. It is the oldest Jewish house of worship still standing in the United States.

Over 100 American Jews fought in the War of Independence. Francis Salvador, was the first to give his life in the cause. Benjamin Nones of New York joined up as a private and rose to the rank of major by the end of the Revolution.

By the time General Washington became President in 1789, there were temples in New York; Newport; Charleston, South Carolina; Savannah, Georgia; and Philadelphia, Pennsylvania. The temple in Newport is called the Touro Synagogue after Judah Touro, a merchant who gave money to complete it. This temple is preserved as a national landmark today.

Through their hard work and loyalty, the first Jews in America proved they were worthy citizens. This made it easier for Jews from other lands to find a place for themselves in the growing country.

Jews from Germany were the next group to come to the United States. They began arriving in 1815, but the largest number came after 1848.

The German Jews settled in all parts of the nation. Many started out as peddlers. A peddler would strap a pack of his wares on his back, and using a stick for balance, he trudged from house to house.

A successful peddler was soon able to buy a horse and wagon. Now he could carry a mountain of wares. The rattle of the peddler's wagon could be heard for miles. Pails dangling from under the wagon clinked together. Pans hanging from a wire stretched across the top of the wagon banged out a message

The Yankee peddler was often a young Jewish immigrant recently arrived from Germany who kept a list of English words by his side to help him talk to customers.

that the peddler was coming. The pioneer family in its lonely homestead could now stock up on needles, pins, cloth, blankets, brooms, mops, nails, and the latest "fancy bonnet" from the workshops of the East.

The next step for the peddler was to settle in a town and open a store. Then his younger brothers continued the traveling. Macy's and Gimbels, two department stores in New York City with many branches in other parts of the country, were built up by the sons and grandsons of these early German tradesmen. Goldwater's, a large department store in Phoenix, Arizona, was founded by Michael Goldwater, who started as a wagon driver. His grandson, Barry Goldwater, was elected to the United States Senate in 1968, and was a Presidential candidate in 1964.

Some peddlers became manufacturers. Levi Strauss arrived in California during the 1849 gold rush. He sold trousers to miners and invented jeans or "Levi's." The San Francisco company he founded sells trousers all over the world today.

Many German Jews settled in Cincinnati, Ohio; Milwaukee, Wisconsin, and other Midwest cities. Some German Jews settled in Baltimore, Maryland, which at one time was a port of entry for immigrants. Others went farther south to Alabama and Georgia.

A few even traveled as far north as Alaska, which then belonged to Russia. Louis Goldstone bought furs from the trappers there for a California trading company. He was the first American to bring back the information that Russia might be interested in selling Alaska. The United States purchased the territory in 1867.

(Left) Levi Strauss, who invented jeans or "Levi's" came to the United States in 1848. (Right) Julius Meyer of Nebraska traded for furs with the Indians. He poses here with his friend Chief Standing Bear of the Ponca tribe.

A few German Jews became bankers in New York and Chicago. They helped other businesses get started. Loans made to young Julius Rosenwald of Chicago helped him enlarge his small company, Sears, Roebuck, until it became a giant mail-order business.

True to the ideals of the Torah, the Jews from Germany set up community services to help their fellow Jews. To provide shelter, they supported homes for orphans and old people. They founded kosher hospitals to keep the kosher laws for the sick. Jews' Hospital, a kosher institution, was opened in New York

City in 1852. Now called Mount Sinai Hospital, it still serves kosher food and also takes care of people of all creeds.

The German Jews started trade schools to teach skills to young people. They opened workshops and training schools for the deaf and blind. Through these schools, every Jew could be taught to take care of himself.

In 1843, twelve German Jews in New York City started a social club for Jewish men called B'nai B'rith, which means "sons of the covenant" or promise. B'nai B'rith grew until it had clubs all over the country. This was one way Jews had of staying in touch with one another.

By 1880, there were about 250,000 Jews in the United States. In the next thirty-five years, the emigration from Russia and Poland would increase their number to over two million! The organizations set up by the Jews from Germany would help this vast number get settled.

When Jacob and his mother arrived in New York, their ship docked at the immigration station at Ellis Island. The station had been opened in 1892 to handle the waves of emigrants coming from Europe. No matter where the newcomer was headed after he landed, he had to pass through Ellis Island. The station officers boasted that they could take care of 5,000 people a day!

Between 1901 and 1910, more immigrants came to the United States than at any other time in history. Almost a million persons entered the country each year. About one in ten were Jews.

The relatives of the arriving immigrants stood on a balcony

A group of immigrants of the 1920s on their arrival in New York City. The Hebrew Immigrant Aid Society (HIAS) would help them settle.

which overlooked the reception building. After a medical examination, the immigrants were led into the building.

As Jacob and his mother filed in, they looked up, trying to spot Tevye. He had written them that he would be waving a bright yellow handkerchief. Jacob saw that people on the baycony were waving small flags and squares of different colors to attract their relatives' attention.

"There, Momma! A man is waving a yellow cloth at us," Jacob cried, pointing toward Tevye.

Mrs. Markowitz smiled and nodded her head. Now she knew everything would be all right.

When their turn came, Tevye vouched for them. The immigration officer took their names, checked their medical cards, and they were free to go.

"He called you 'Max'," Mrs. Markowitz said to Tevye, after they left the officer.

"That's my name now," Max-born-Tevye told her. He explained that he had been given the name "Max" by an immigration officer, when he first came to the United States. "I couldn't speak English, and he didn't understand what I was saying. Many immigrants have had their names changed in this way." However, their names in Hebrew remained the same.

Max took Mrs. Markowitz and Jacob to a ferry that crossed the bay to Manhattan, a borough of New York City. Then they took a streetcar to the lower East Side, where Max and Ida lived.

The lower East Side covered about one hundred blocks of land, bordering on the East River. Fifty years before, Irish immigrants had lived in this part of the city. Now most of them had moved uptown to newer housing. The places they left had been taken by other immigrant groups.

In 1905, the eastern European Jews were the largest group on the lower East Side. Like other immigrant groups, they wanted to live together when they first came to the United States. They felt more at home living with one another in the new land. As many as three thousand people lived on one block. They were squeezed into small apartments in five- and six-story wood and brick buildings.

Most of the buildings were old. The only heat came from coal stoves in the kitchens. The building in which Jacob was to live had no inside bathrooms. Five outhouses in the rear yard served the 250 people of this building. Children were bathed in washtubs in the kitchen. The adults went to bathhouses in

A combined bath and laundry in a tenement sink on the lower East Side in the early 1900s.

the neighborhood. The bathhouses contained steam rooms and showers. These were run by the city and were free.

Crowded conditions like these existed in other cities also. Immigrants flocked to places where housing was cheap and they could find work easily. In Chicago, Jews lived on the West Side of town; in Philadelphia, they lived in the downtown area; and in Boston, they lived in the northern end of the city.

Jewish agencies such as the Hebrew Immigrant Aid Society (HIAS) tried to help the newcomer settle in less-crowded areas. HIAS offered to pay the immigrant's fare to the Middle West or upstate New York. As a result, communities of Jewish immigrants could be found in smaller American cities, too.

Other agencies tried to settle them on farms. But many of the farmers gave up and returned to the cities. Some turned their farms into summer guesthouses which later became large hotels in the Catskill area of New York. Many New Jersey egg and chicken farmers today are children and grandchildren of these immigrants. One Jewish farmer in Maine became the largest potato grower there.

Yet, despite the efforts to spread the newcomers out, most of them clung to the cities. And for them, the way of life would be very much the same as it was for Jacob.

As he and his mother stepped down from the trolley with Max, they joined the throng of people on the lower East Side. They were on Hester Street, the neighborhood shopping center. Pushcarts lined the street on both sides. From the carts people

Jewish organizations tried to help immigrants settle on farms or in smaller towns away from the crowded cities. These Jewish farmers of 1913 are attending a dinner.

Hester Street, the local shopping center, in 1898. Jacob's apartment house was like those in this scene.

were buying fish, bolts of cloth, all kinds of food and clothing, and even eyeglasses.

Max urged them on. There were several more blocks to go before they reached Essex Street where they would be living.

Finally they were in front of their building. "This is number 147," Max said.

Jacob saw the numbers painted in black on the worn, wooden door of a soot-stained, brick building which was squeezed between others just like it. They would live on the fifth and top floor.

Inside, they climbed the rickety stairs. The only light came from a gas lamp on each landing.

"Your sister Ida and I have two children," Max said to Jacob as they rested part of the way up. "The baby is called Sarah. Our son, David, is almost five. He is your nephew, but since you are almost the same age, you will share a room and be good friends."

They began climbing again, and suddenly Jacob saw a lighted doorway ahead. A sandy-haired chubby boy gazed down at him. This was David. Behind David stood Ida, as well as several neighbors who had lived in the same town as the Markowitz family in the "old country."

Laughing and shouting, the people inside the apartment made way for the travelers. Jacob was hugged and kissed as he passed from person to person. Finally, he and David went to their room.

"Are there cossacks in America?" Jacob whispered when they were alone.

"What are cossacks?" David answered. "I never heard of them!"

Jacob smiled as he looked around the small room he would share with his nephew. The room had no window, and the wide bed filled up most of the space. But Jacob knew that he was safe, and he was happy.

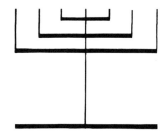

CHAPTER FOUR

Home and School

"KEEP WARM!" Mrs. Markowitz called after Jacob and David as they left the apartment for school.

"Eat more!" and "Keep warm!" were her favorite words. These instructions were the best way she knew of keeping them all healthy. Any illness would be a danger to the three adults and three children who lived in the three-room apartment.

Mrs. Markowitz slept on a cot in the kitchen. To give the boys a good start each day, she was up early. She lit the coal stove and warmed the boys' clothing near it. Then she gave each of them a glass of hot tea and milk, followed by a bowl of steaming oatmeal. She saw that they were bundled into coats, scarves, caps, and mittens before they left for school.

Education held first place in the mind of the immigrant Jew, as well as the Jews of all times and places. They were commanded by the Torah to teach its 613 laws to their children. Only by learning to read and write could the children learn the laws and understand them.

But to the Jews, education meant even more in America. It was a chance to get ahead, to find out what one could do best. In the United States it was possible to study for any kind of job. It was possible also to study just for the pure joy of learning, because libraries and free schools were available to all.

Jacob had been taught to read Hebrew in Europe. Mrs. Markowitz was so anxious for him to learn that she put a dab of honey on the inside cover of his first book. Jacob tasted the honey and thought the book was good. Jewish parents hoped that this good feeling about books would carry over to all books.

At first Jacob went to school on a boat tied up to a dock on the East River. There were so many children in the area that the old boat had to be used until a new school was built.

Jacob struggled in school. The language was new and so was the alphabet. He had to learn to read from left to right. But after a while, the strange letters and words began to make sense to him.

By the time David was ready for school, the boys could go to one in a regular building a block from their house.

Each day after school was over at three o'clock, the boys rushed home. The apartment was empty. The two mothers were earning the money they needed by sewing clothing in a neighbor's apartment. They took Sarah with them. The boys found money and a shopping list on the kitchen table.

Now they went into action on a system they had worked out

Boys and girls did not sit together in this crowded classroom. The desks pulled down for writing. Light came from two gas jets hanging from the ceiling, and heat came from the stove in the corner.

to make their chore easier. Jacob dashed downstairs to the store. Meanwhile, David got a cloth bag ready; it had a long laundry cord tied to the top. When he heard Jacob calling, he opened the kitchen window and let the bag down to the street. Jacob filled the bag with the groceries and tied the top. Then David hauled it up.

As soon as the groceries were put away, David came downstairs carrying their Hebrew books. In a few minutes they were due at Hebrew school. Munching apples, or pieces of coarse rye bread, they hurried along.

The Hebrew school was called a Talmud Torah, a place to learn the "law." Sitting on benches in a small narrow room, the boys also studied how to read and write Hebrew.

Some students went to a Yeshiva, an all-day school. Yeshiva means sitting, and the students did a lot of sitting in these schools. They studied Hebrew subjects until three o'clock and then subjects in English until seven. These schools went to the eighth grade, although a few also offered high school subjects. Graduates of the high schools could go on to academies of higher Hebrew learning. One of these academies later became Yeshiva University in New York City.

Boys are studying with the rabbi, who is a teacher of the Jewish faith. The Talmud, the book they are reading, tells about the Hebrew laws.

The religious schools charged what the parents could afford to pay. This was usually not enough to cover the costs. The difference was made up by donations of "uptown Jews," those who had already made enough money to move away from the lower East Side.

Mrs. Markowitz went to school also, two nights a week. She wanted to become an American citizen, and to do so she had to learn English.

Max was an ironworker. For ten hours each day, he bolted iron railings onto the staircases of new buildings. Max was weary at night, but once a week after dinner, he struggled into his hat and jacket to go to a meeting.

Max belonged to a club called the Workmen's Circle. The men in his branch were from his hometown in Russia. They paid dues and voted on how the money could be used. The Circle was a kind of insurance plan. It paid small sums of money to members and their families who became ill or died. The Jewish immigrants brought these self-help ideas with them from the pale and the ghettos of Europe. These ideas led to the government programs of hospital care and Social Security that Americans now enjoy.

The Jewish newspapers helped the immigrant adjust to life in America. In many ways, the newspapers were the eyes, ears, and heart of the Jewish community. They were printed in Yiddish, the language all eastern European Jews could understand.

Yiddish is a form of German. It is written using Hebrew letters. Since almost every Jew could read Hebrew, he could also read Yiddish. Magazines, books, and six newspapers were published in Yiddish in Chicago and in New York City on the lower East Side.

Max brought home the *Jewish Daily Forward* each night. The paper carried local and national news, as well as announcements of meetings and jobs. It published names of new arrivals who were looking for their relatives. But the best part of the paper was the section that carried the stories of Yiddish writers like Sholom Aleichem. The boys hurried through their chore of drying dishes so they could find out what happened in the next chapter of the current story. In later years, the papers published the stories of Isaac Bashevis Singer. These tales have since been translated into English. Those of Sholom Aleichem have also been made into the long-running Broadway play "Fiddler on the Roof."

The *Tageblatt* or *Jewish Daily News* was another Yiddish paper. Mrs. Sarasohn, the publisher's wife, tried to help the immigrant boys. Secretly, she gave them free copies of the paper when they passed the back door of the newspaper building. The paper sold for a penny, and at the end of the day each boy usually had a profit of a few cents. This meant he could buy a bag of Indian nuts, or a baked sweet potato, or a glass of seltzer called "two cents plain."

The Jews on the lower East Side also had their own theater. Plays were performed in Yiddish each weekend. A good play went on tour to other cities which had a Yiddish-speaking population. Whole families, including babies, went to the theater together. They ate pretzels and candy, and drank soft drinks

A scene from "Fiddler on the Roof." Tevye, the father in the play, is a poor Russian Jew. Because of the Czar, the Jews are in constant danger, like the fiddler perched on the roof. The play is based on the Yiddish stories of Sholom Aleichem. In the early 1900s, American plays were translated into Yiddish. Today, it is the other way around.

while they watched the show. Even though the immigrant had not yet learned English, he could take part in American life through his publications and plays.

The coffeehouse was another landmark of Jewish neighborhoods. Here Jews would sit hour after hour, arguing passionately about many things. The subject might be the latest Yiddish play, the President of the United States; business, or a point of Jewish law.

All week long, night and day, the immigrant was busy working. He had to work to remain alive. But the goal of a better life for his children helped to keep his spirits up. Through his schools and clubs, he felt he was running his own affairs. This made him work hard. But on Friday night, the long week of work came to a close. The Sabbath was about to begin. Friday night in Jewish homes is still the high spot of the week.

On Friday morning there was a feeling of gaiety on Hester Street, as people rushed around preparing for the Sabbath. Jacob and David did not have classes at the Talmud Torah on Friday afternoon, so they helped with Sabbath preparations. David was set to work polishing the brass candlesticks. He had heard the story of how his grandmother had hidden her candlesticks in her bundle when she escaped from Russia. He took special care to make them gleam. Jacob was sent downstairs to buy some last-minute supplies from the peddlers, who soon would put away their pushcarts.

Men left work early on Friday. They went to the public bathhouses and then came home. By four o'clock, usually noisy Hester Street had quieted down.

The home looked different on this day, too. In the kitchen, Mrs. Markowitz put a while cloth over the shiny oilcloth that usually covered the table. Four brightly polished candlesticks (two belonged to Ida) were on a tray on the table. Each candlestick held a small white candle.

The candles were lit by the mothers of the house before sundown. Bowing their heads and holding their hands out to encircle the flickering flames, Ida and Mrs. Markowitz said a prayer.

Now the whole family gathered around the table for dinner. First Max filled a cup with wine and said a prayer over it. The wine was another sign that the Sabbath was a special time. Then Max said a blessing over the *challah,* the special Sabbath bread.

Ida and Mrs. Markowitz scrimped all week to make the

Jewish women of yesterday and today recite the same words: "Blessed art Thou, O Lord our God, King of the Universe, who hast sanctified us by Thy laws and commanded us to kindle the Sabbath light."

Sabbath meal as grand as any family could afford. But every family on the lower East Side was sure of having a good meal because of the Sabbath fund. Families contributed to this fund at their temples.

At Jacob's house, the dinner started with gelfilte (stuffed) fish. It was made of chopped white fish, and egg, matzoh meal, carrots, and onions were added. The mixture was shapped into a ball and boiled. The fish balls were served hot or cold, with a spoonful of sharp horseradish which made Jacob's eyes tear. The horseradish gave the fish a spicy taste. Today, gefilte fish can be bought in cans or jars in many stores.

Next came chicken soup with golden noodles floating in it. This was followed by steaming chicken served with a side dish of sweet potatoes mixed with prunes and carrots and cooked in a sugar syrup. Homemade nut cake and tea completed the meal.

All this food made everyone sleepy. But the family stayed at the table reading or talking, and munching on nuts and raisins. Soon someone would notice that David was asleep in his chair.

Max carried him to bed, with Jacob trailing behind. The following morning the family would have to be up early to go to the temple, which they called *shul*.

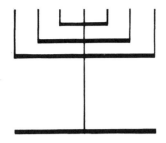

CHAPTER FIVE

Holidays and Celebrations

When Max and the boys arrived at temple on Saturday morning, people were already at prayer. The men wore white prayer shawls draped over their shoulder. On the back of their heads they had small round black *yarmulkes,* the Polish word for cap. Women sat at the sides of the room, separated from the men by a curtain. They were hidden so they would not distract the men from prayers. Orthodox temples today are very much like this one.

As they prayed, men and women rocked back and forth slightly. A low murmuring could be heard as they read the Hebrew words. The prayers were led by a cantor, who chanted the melody. Sometimes the cantor looked up, as if he were speaking to God. His song begged for help for suffering people everywhere. The haunting chants touched Jacob. Sometimes he felt like crying out too as he heard the cantor's mournful tones. When the song ended, everyone said "Amen," may it be so.

In the early 1900s there were over 300 Orthodox temples, like the one to which Max belonged, on the lower East Side. Every city had small temples like these, in storefronts, in apartment houses, or in tiny brick buildings. Today these small temples have dwindled, as people moved away to new areas. Larger Orthodox synagogues have been built in the major American cities.

Orthodox Judaism is one of three main branches of the Jewish faith in the United States. There are two other branches: Conservative and Reform Judaism.

Reform, or Liberal, Judaism was introduced in the United States in the early 1800s by the Jews from Germany where the movement started. The first Reform temple was in Charleston, South Carolina, but Cincinnati, Ohio, where many German Jews settled, became a center for this movement. A college for the training of Reform rabbis is located there, as well as in New York City and Los Angeles.

The early Reform Jews hoped to make the ancient traditions have meaning to Jews who had lost touch with their religion when they came to America. These Jews had not learned Hebrew so they could not understand the Orthodox service. Therefore, Reform Jews prayed in English as well as Hebrew so everyone could understand the words. This still holds true today. In addition, men and women may sit together at services. There is no chanting, but worshippers read together from the prayer

50

book. A choir and an organ provide the music. Reform Jews are not required to keep the kosher laws or wear yarmulkes in temple, but they may do so if they wish.

Conservative Judaism was born in the United States. Its aims are to "conserve" Jewish traditions while making them fit American life. The Jewish Theological Seminary in New York trains Conservative rabbis, and sponsors New York City's Jewish Museum. It also has a vast library of Hebrew books and scrolls which are used by the world's scholars.

In all branches of Judaism, the rabbi is the religious leader of the temple or synagogue. Rabbis are not assigned to their posts. The members of each temple hire their own rabbi. Together they decide just how to carry out the many customs of conducting temple services. For this reason, temples sometimes differ in forms of worship.

Although there are differences, all Jews share the ideals of the Torah, as well as the same holidays and celebrations.

The holidays have always been an enriching part of Jewish life. And the custom of Bar Mitzvah has always been a favorite occasion for celebration. Bar Mitzvah means "Son of the Commandment." At thirteen, a boy may become a Bar Mitzvah. A girl may be a Bas Mitzvah—that is, a "Daughter of the Commandment." The Bar Mitzvah promises to keep the commandments and be responsible for what he does throughout his life.

When Jacob became a Bar Mitzvah, he was called to the altar of his synagogue to read from the Torah. He had prepared for this day by studying with the rabbi and by learning to chant

On the Saturday after
his thirteenth birthday,
this young man was
called to the altar to
become a Bar Mitzvah.

from the cantor. He also wrote a speech in Yiddish which he read to the worshippers. In the speech, Jacob told about the meaning of the portion of the Torah he had read.

After the services, Mrs. Markowitz invited the congregation to have lunch in another room of the little yellow brick temple. She, Ida, and some of their neighbors had made all kinds of cold fish dishes, breads, and cakes. The adults toasted Jacob with sweet kosher wine. "Mazel tov!" they said. "Good luck."

"Were you scared?" David wanted to know when he and Jacob were alone.

"Not after I got started," said Jacob grinning.

The Jewish holidays are welcome occasions also because at these times families come together. One such holiday is Rosh Hashanah, which means "Beginning of the Year." This holiday falls in September or October.

The dates on which all Jewish holidays fall are based on the Jewish calendar. The date of the beginning of the world was figured out by scholars from information in the Bible. That date is 3760 B.C. If you add this figure to the present year in our calendar, you will get the present year in the Jewish calendar.

Rosh Hashanah starts the ten-day period called the High Holy Days. Jews think about their deeds during the past year. If they have done anything wrong, they will try to make up for it. They hope to pay back debts and they ask forgiveness from man and God.

A special symbol of Rosh Hashanah is the sounding of the shofar, or ram's horn. The shepherds of ancient days used the horn to call to each other. The clear haunting sound reminds each person in the temple to "sound" out his own thoughts.

The shofar or curved ram's horn.

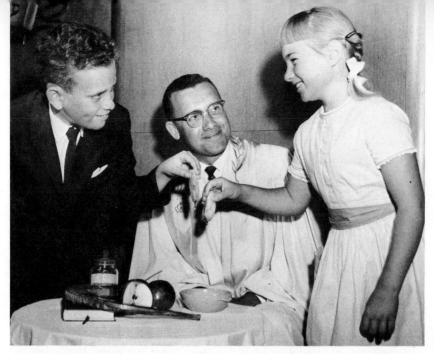

Here are three symbols of Rosh Hashanah. The boy and girl dip the apple in honey to wish each other "a sweet year." Rabbi Herman watching them, wears white robes in honor of the holiday. The curved ram's horn he will blow rests on the table.

Ten days after Rosh Hashanah, the most holy day in the Jewish year arrives. This day is called Yom Kippur, the Day of Atonement.

On Yom Kippur, Jews fast as a way of "atoning" for sins they may have committed. The fast lasts from dusk on Yom Kippur eve until prayers are completed late the following day. When the prayers are over, the shofar is sounded once more. Families stream home from temple, tired and hungry, but hopeful that a good year lies ahead.

Children and ill or very elderly people are not required to fast. Many Reform Jews fast only part of the day.

Four days after Yom Kippur, another holiday arrives. It is Sukkoth, or the Festival of the Tabernacles. Sukkoth and tabernacle are other words for huts, booths, or temporary houses. The Bible says the roofs of the Sukkoth must be left open. The Jews of ancient times put up huts with open roofs as they wandered in the desert after their escape from slavery in Egypt.

American Jews today remember this event by building booths in some open area of their synagogues or in the yards of their homes. Since the holiday also celebrates the harvest, the booths are hung with fruits and vegetables. Thanksgiving, begun by the Pilgrims, was modeled on what they read about Sukkoth in their Bibles.

In New York City today, there is little room to build a Sukkah for each family. The sisterhood of Temple B'nai Jeshurun hangs grapes, carrots, pears, strings of cranberry, other fruits, and flowers in the community Sukkah on the roof of their temple.

The Sukkoth festival lasts eight days. The final day is called Simhath Torah, the Rejoicing of the Law. This is the day that the last chapter of the Torah scroll is read. At that same service, the scroll is rewound and the reading is started again. In this way, the Jew demonstrates that thought and life go on.

The festival of Hanukkah takes place in December. Its symbol is the Menorah, an eight-branched candleholder. Hanukkah is Hebrew for "dedication." Hanukkah reminds Jews of the reopening of their ancient temple after it had been looted and defiled by the ruler Antiochus Epiphanes.

Legend says that only a drop of oil remained in the lamp in the rebuilt temple. This lamp must never be permitted to go out, but no oil could be found for eight days. By a miracle, the drop of oil continued burning all that time!

It is the last night of Hanukkah. A child uses the "shamos" or servant candle to light all the others. Her sister watches.

At the Passover Seder, the youngest child wants to know: "Why is this night different from all other nights?" Then he asks the Four Questions: "On all other nights we eat bread or matzohs; on this night, why only matzohs? On all other nights we eat herbs of any kind; on this night, why only bitter herbs? On all other nights we do not dip our herbs even once; on this night, why do we dip them twice? On all other nights we eat our meals in any manner; on this night, why do we recline on pillows?"

The answers are read from the Haggadah. Some of the symbols of Passover, which are explained in the Haggadah, can be seen on the plate on the table. The matzoh is on one dish. The other holds a lamb bone, an egg, horse radish (bitter herbs) chopped apples and nuts in wine, and parsley in salt water for dipping.

To remember this event, American Jews light a candle each night for eight nights. Boys and girls take turns adding a new candle each night, and replacing the burned-out ones. After the candles are blessed and lit each evening, the children are given a small gift by their parents. Some American Jews place an electric candleholder in their windows during the festival. Each night they turn on another light.

Another day for the giving of gifts is Purim. This holiday tells how Queen Esther saved the Jews in Persia from an evil man called Haman.

The holiday of Passover is celebrated in the spring. During the eight days of Passover, Jews may eat no bread. Instead, they eat matzohs, which looks like a large cracker. Matzohs reminds Jews of the time they fled from slavery in Egypt.

In their hurry to escape, they had to take food that could be made quickly. The dough for making bread contains yeast, which takes too long to rise. Since there is no yeast in matzohs, the dough does not have to rise, so it was taken instead.

Matzohs are still eaten today. They can be bought year-round in many supermarkets. However, for use during the Passover holiday, matzohs are specially prepared.

Passover starts with a special service in the home called a Seder. The family reads from the Haggadah, a small book that tells the story of the Jews' fight to win their freedom. The Jews read this story every year so that they will always value their freedom and remember to protect it. "For in every generation," the Haggadah warns, "nations rise against us and seek our destruction."

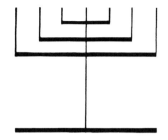

CHAPTER SIX

Earning a Living

"KNISHES! GET YOUR HOT KNISHES!" sang out the man on the corner. The "k" is pronounced in knishes, which are small flaky pastries filled with potatoes or groats. The man was turning them slowly on his stove. In 1900, he sold them two for a penny.

The kind of work many Jews performed in the United States was linked to their heritage. Thousands made or sold kosher food to their fellow Jews; many still do.

Kosher butcher shops could be found wherever Jews lived in any number. Groceries and bakeries, run by Jews, sold American as well as Jewish specialties. Some bakeries specialized only in bagels. These look like doughnuts but are eaten in place of bread or rolls. To make a favorite Jewish sandwich, bagels are sliced and spread with cream cheese and slices of pink smoked salmon called lox.

Jewish-Americans opened hardware stores, laundries, and dry cleaning stores. They kept general stores, shoe shops, and tailor shops. In Europe, keeping shop had been one of the few kinds of work open to Jews. Families there lived behind the store, and everyone worked in it. Now, in the United States, the same pattern was followed.

Shopkeepers who observed the Sabbath laws remained closed on Saturdays. They were open on Sunday instead.

By 1906, New York City subway lines were operating from Manhattan into the boroughs of the Bronx and Brooklyn. New housing sprang up around each subway station. Those who could now afford better housing moved uptown to Harlem and the Bronx, or out to the tree-lined avenues of Brooklyn. Painters, carpenters, and plumbers were needed to work on the new buildings. Many Jews worked in these trades.

The production of Jewish foods provides jobs for Jewish and non-Jewish workers. This factory makes matzohs the year-round.

But most Jewish-Americans worked at manufacturing, in what is known as the needle trades. They made hats and caps, fur garments, knitted goods, and clothing of all kinds.

One hundred years ago, at the end of the Civil War, workshops sprang up in many cities for the manufacture of coats, suits, dresses, and blouses. These small factories employed from six to twenty people who worked for very low wages. Immigrants took these jobs willingly.

The small workshops, often located in the employer's home, fit the needs of the Jewish immigrant. He didn't have to know English to work in one, and if his employer was Jewish, the newcomer could continue to keep the Sabbath laws. Later, he could even open his own workshop, with his wife and children and some neighbors as helpers. This is the kind of shop Mrs. Markowitz and Ida worked at in their building on Essex Street.

The small factories were busiest in summer. That was when clothing for fall and winter was made. The poorly lit rooms were crowded and miserably hot in summer. That is why they were called sweatshops.

Workers were paid by the number of garments the whole shop completed. This was called the task system. Everyone worked frantically, from dawn until late evening, to see the pile of finished garments grow.

As the weather got cooler, there was less for the bosses and workers to do. They "sweated" then too. They worried that their earnings would stop completely.

By 1910, some of the small workshops had grown into large factories. A few of the factories employed as many as 2,500

Sweatshops were crowded, poorly lighted, and the danger of fire was always present. Here men, women, and children are working together.

workers. Conditions in the larger factories were not much better than in the small ones. During the busy season, all workers were required to be at their sewing machines seven days a week.

"If you don't come in Sunday, don't come in Monday!" the boss would warn his workers. He meant that anyone who took Sunday off would be fired.

The factories were not always safe. Because a stairway door was bolted, 147 persons, mostly young girls, lost their lives in a fire that destroyed the Triangle shirtwaist factory, in 1911.

Since the 1880s, workers had been trying to improve their

A modern garment factory. Proper lighting, clean air, and the security of a weekly wage help the workers do a good job.

working conditions. They joined labor unions to press demands for better wages, shorter hours, and safer places to work.

Jewish garment workers played an important role in the labor union movement. Two important labor union leaders were Jewish immigrants from Russia and Poland.

Sidney Hillman arrived in Chicago in 1896. He was nineteen, and found a factory job making men's suits. A few years later, he was a union official. He was able to show manufacturers how improved conditions of work would benefit both owners and workers. Sidney Hillman served as president of the Amalgamated

63

Clothing Workers of America for thirty-two years. He helped found the huge Congress of Industrial Organizations (CIO). He was an advisor to Presidents Franklin D. Roosevelt and Harry S. Truman.

David Dubinsky, a Polish immigrant, learned to be a cutter in New York City. Using a special machine, he sliced through layers of cloth, cutting out the pieces of fabric from which garments would be made. He joined the International Ladies Garment Workers Union (ILGWU) and later became its president.

Under Dubinsky's forceful leadership, the ILGWU won higher wages for its workers, and eventually a five-day week. The union taught skills to new workers so they could move into better jobs in the industry.

At the present time, a large number of needle trades workers are Jewish. But many are Puerto Ricans and blacks from the southern states who have migrated to New York City.

The children of the Jewish immigrants were educated in many different trades and skills. They did not take their parents' places at the sewing machines and cutting tables. Some, like Jacob, struggled through college at night to earn degrees. But during the 1920s, Jewish-Americans often found that jobs in large American companies were closed to them.

They were aware that there had always been some prejudice against Jews in the United States. Freedom of religion was the law of the land, but many Americans were of European background. They brought their prejudice against Jews with them when they came to America. Others wanted to keep Jews out of certain industries because they feared all newcomers. They were afraid that the Jews would compete for their jobs, want to move into their neighborhoods, join their clubs, and enter their schools.

Colleges had quotas or limits on the number of Jews that could be admitted. For many years it was very hard for a Jew to enter medical school because of these quotas. Hotels also had signs that read: "No dogs or Jews allowed." A southern organization called the Ku Klux Klan burned crosses on the lawns of Jewish homes. Other hate groups declared that no more Jews should be allowed to come to the United States.

In 1913, B'nai B'rith had started the Anti-Defamation League (ADL) to try to bring the true facts about American Jews to other Americans. They tried to work with employers to open up jobs to qualified Jews. But progress was slow. There were no laws against discrimination in jobs at that time.

College-educated Jews turned to other fields for employment. Jacob became a social worker. Many others became teachers or government employees. In these fields, ability was the first consideration.

After 1929 jobs were scarce for all Americans. It was a time known as the Great Depression. Factories closed and people wandered the streets looking for work.

The depression gripped Europe, too. In Germany, a tyrant named Adolf Hitler rose to power in 1933. He had a program for creating jobs for his people and making Germany the world's most powerful nation. First, he planned to eliminate the German Jews and to keep their valuable property. Jews were once again required to wear a yellow badge as a mark that they were Jewish. Respected Jews were taken away in the night and never heard from again.

It did not seem possible that the mass murder of a people could take place in the modern world. But it was true. Jews by the thousands were herded into cattle cars, and taken to concentration camps. There they were marched into gas-filled rooms to their death.

American Jews knew what was happening in Europe from the letters they received from their relatives. They pleaded with their own government to allow these Jews to escape to the United States. But no country in the world would take more than a few thousand.

In 1921, the United States had put a limit on the number of immigrants that would be admitted from any one country. Only about 20,000 European Jews could enter the United States each

German army photo of Nazi soldiers rounding up Jewish families in Warsaw, Poland, in 1939.

year, because the quotas from their countries were low.

American Jews sent money to Europe to resettle Jews in South America, Canada, Palestine, China, or any place that would take them. Then in 1939, Germany attacked other countries in Europe, and World War II began.

When the United States entered the war in 1941, Jewish-Americans enlisted in great numbers, along with other Americans. Germany was beaten by 1945. Then the awful accounting was made. Millions of people of all countries and faiths had lost

At left, a newspaper cartoon of the period. Many Americans wanted the door to immigration opened for the European victims of the Nazi holocaust.

Below, thousands were saved. These Jewish children from Europe were cared for in American homes. European Christians helped many Jewish families by hiding them on their farms or in their homes until the war was over.

their lives. But Europe's Jews had almost been wiped out. Of the ten million Jews who lived in Europe before the war, less than four million survived. Six million Jews had been murdered!

Even though many years have passed, the holocaust, as Jews call the German tragedy, is still very real to the Jews in the United States. Almost every Jewish-American family lost some European relatives in the slaughter. European Jews, now in America, still bear the scars of the prison camps. Some men and women always wear long sleeves to cover the purple prison numbers tattoed forever on their arms.

After the war, Americans felt great sympathy for the Jews in their own country and elsewhere. The United States was one of the first governments to recognize the reestablishment of the country of Israel. This tiny piece of land in Asia became a haven for the homeless Jews of the world. Americans of all faiths contributed money to help the new country get started.

A farm worker in Israel. The numbers on his arm were put there at the Nazi death camp from which he was rescued.

In the United States, prejudice against Jews lessened. Jobs opened up for American Jews in all industries. They were accepted in sections of towns that once had laws to keep them out. Colleges no longer asked the religion of an applicant. Jews could compete on the same basis as everyone else.

After the war, American business surged forward. Jewish-Americans had always been drawn to new business ideas. There was no discrimination on the ground floor of a new industry; whoever was willing to take a chance was welcome.

As early as 1910, Louis B. Mayer saw that movie-making could one day become a worldwide industry. He formed a company for making films that still bears his name. It is MGM, Metro-Goldwyn-Mayer.

David Sarnoff, who came from Russia as a young boy, started work at fifteen as a telegraph operator. He understood that the new science of electronics could make radio broadcasting available to all. As president of the Radio Corporation of America (RCA), he led his company to develop radio, black and white television and color television. RCA has also provided electronic equipment for the space program.

Edwin H. Land was working on new product ideas even while a student at Harvard College. He invented the Polaroid camera. After the war, Dr. Land turned his idea into a vast new industry.

The newer Jewish-Americans, those who were refugees from Europe during the 1940s, put the skills they brought with them to work. They opened candy and bake shops featuring European recipes. Diamond cutters from Belgium were needed in jewelry

At fifteen, David Sarnoff taught himself the Morse code and became a telegraph operator. In the picture above, he is shown at work on Nantucket Island. Below, fifty-two years later, David Sarnoff meets with New York's Senator Jacob Javits and the then Vice-President Lyndon Johnson.

workshops. American universities welcomed scientists and professors from France, Germany, and Austria.

Many Jewish-Americans also took part in the building boom all over America. Samuel Lefrak, of New York, constructed thousands of apartment houses. Bertram Goldberg designed Marina Towers in Chicago. But most Jewish-Americans worked in the building trades as plumbers, electricians, and painters. Many others were secretaries, typists, clerks, accountants, and salesmen in businesses of all kinds.

In many ways, Americans of the Jewish faith helped their country grow.

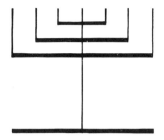

CHAPTER SEVEN

Contributors in Science, Government, and the Arts

JEWISH-AMERICANS have also performed deeds which have benefited mankind. A number of men and women have been important in medicine.

Joseph Goldberger became a medical doctor, despite the poverty he lived in on the lower East Side. By rising at four in the morning, young Joseph was able to study in quiet in his crowded apartment. His parents, brother, and sisters pooled their meager earnings to pay for medical school. Joseph Goldberger became a doctor for the United States Public Health Service. Time and again he risked his life by experimenting on himself. But in the end he found that the lack of one vitamin was the cause of pellagra, a skin disease that affected many people in the southern part of the country.

Doctors Albert Sabin and Jonas Salk were responsible for the vaccines that have nearly wiped out the crippling disease polio. Dr. Sabin, who was born in Poland in 1906, now does research at the Children's Hospital Research Foundation in Cincinnati. Dr. Salk heads the Salk Institute for Biological Studies in San Diego, California.

In 1902, nurse Lillian Wald and her Christian friend, nurse Mary Brewster, went to live and work among the poor on the lower East Side. This two-woman Peace Corps started the Henry Street Settlement Nursing Service. The Settlement House also gave free music and art lessons to children. Miss Wald also began the school nurse program.

In the field of science, one of the most outstanding names is that of Albert Einstein. Born in Germany, Dr. Einstein fled his native land and in 1933 came to the United States. He had won

Dr. Jonas E. Salk

Justice Louis D. Brandeis

the Nobel Prize in Physics in 1921. The 1969 Nobel Prize in Physics was awarded to Dr. Murray Gell-Mann of the California Institute of Technology.

Jewish-Americans have also been active in the field of law and government. Five of them have served on the Supreme Court, the highest court in the land: Louis D. Brandeis, Benjamin Cardozo, Felix Frankfurter, Arthur Goldberg, and Abraham Fortas. Justice Brandeis was the first Jewish-American to be appointed to this post. He was born in Kentucky. Brandeis University in Waltham, Massachusetts, is named in his honor.

Jack Greenberg, a New York lawyer, has argued many civil rights cases before the Supreme Court. He is the director of the Legal Defense and Education Fund of the National Association

Arthur J. Goldberg

for the Advancement of Colored People. Mr. Greenberg presented and helped win the school desegregation case before the Supreme Court in 1954.

Jewish-Americans have been elected to public office since 1775 when Francis Salvador became an assemblyman in South Carolina. Today, Emanuel Celler of Brooklyn is called the dean of the House of Representatives in Washington. He has been in Congress since 1922. Jacob Javits, New York's senior senator, was born on the lower East Side in 1904.

American Jews are major contributors to American literature. Their books cover the struggles of Jews in America, but they also write about the problems of man today. Jewish authors have written books on science, art, history, humor and poetry. Emma

76

Leonard Bernstein

Lazarus, a poet, lived in the 1800s. She is most famous for her poem "The New Colossus," which is reproduced at the base of the Statue of Liberty. In 1949, playwright Arthur Miller won the Pulitzer Drama Prize for his play "Death of a Salesman." In 1967, Bernard Malamud won the Pulitzer Prize in Letters for his book *The Fixer.*

Jewish-Americans have contributed many names to the world of music. Leonard Bernstein was born in Boston in 1919. He is a composer and conductor. His concerts for children have been on television. He wrote the music for the play "West Side Story." Among outstanding performers is Beverly Sills, of the New York State Opera Company. Her grandfather was a cantor in Europe, and Miss Sills, who was born in Brooklyn, has performed in

77

Beverly Sills

Europe also. Jan Peerce, Robert Merrill, and Richard Tucker are all Metropolitan Opera stars. During the High Holy Days, Richard Tucker still returns to his synagogue as cantor.

Many Jewish-Americans are well known as philanthropists—that is "lovers of their fellowmen" because they have given large sums of money to worthy causes. Since the country began, they have helped their neighbors. In colonial times, Haym Salomon gave funds for the building of a temple and a church in Philadelphia. In 1840, Judah Touro supplied the money needed to finish the Bunker Hill monument in Boston. Nathan Straus of New York started a free milk fund in 1892. At centers all over the city, free pasteurized milk was given out.

Julius Rosenwald and his family gave funds to build over

4,000 schools for black Americans after the Civil War. He also aided Tuskegee Institute in Alabama and founded Chicago's Museum of Industry.

Jacob Schiff aided the Henry Street Settlement and donated funds to make Ellis Island more comfortable for arriving immigrants. The Guggenheim family set up scholarships for scholars and artists which permit them to study and travel abroad. This family also built the Guggenheim Museum of Art in New York City. Herbert H. Lehman was governor of New York State for five terms, and later became a United States senator. His parting gift to the city he loved was the Children's Zoo in New York's Central Park.

Senator and Mrs. Lehman and their guests at the opening of the Children's Zoo in New York City.

The Jewish comedian has been an important bridge between the American and Jewish cultures. Perhaps because Jews have had troubles, they have always had a sense of humor. They felt better when they laughed at poverty and persecution. But all peoples have troubles, and so Jewish humor has come to have meaning for them, too.

During the early days of radio and movies, the Jew was often shown as a pitiful stranger with a funny accent. But today's comedian plays a different role. He talks about his childhood and culture with warmth and respect. He uses Jewish words like "kosher" and "nudnick" (a pest) and people laugh with him and use these words, too. Through his jokes and stories, the Jewish comedian has spread an understanding of Jewish life in America. Some well-known Jewish comedians are Buddy Hackett, Sam Levenson, and Alan King.

Jews have also made their mark in the sports world. Barney Ross and Benny Leonard became boxing champions. In baseball,

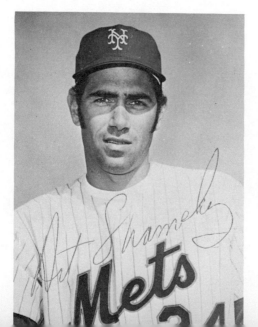

Art Shamsky

Dean Hiltzik

outfielder Hank Greenberg starred with the Detroit Tigers, and Sandy Koufax pitched the Los Angeles Dodgers to many victories. Mike Epstein plays for the Washington Senators and Art Shamsky is with the New York Mets.

Dean Hiltzik of Westbury, New York, was the 1968 Novice Figure Skating Champion of the United States at fourteen. In 1970 he won the Eastern Junior Men's title. Mark Spitz of California captured an Olympic swimming medal for the United States in 1968. Mark and his fifteen-year-old sister Nancy also won medals in 1969 when they represented the United States at the Maccabiah Games in Israel.

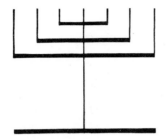

CHAPTER EIGHT

The American Jew Today

THE LOWER EAST SIDE today is still a colorful area. On Sunday afternoons people come from all over to shop. They visit the kosher delicatessens, buy Jewish religious articles, or purchase bargains in clothing from the stores that still line some of the streets.

The pushcarts on Hester Street are gone, but a man selling knishes can usually be found. Some of the old buildings have been replaced by new apartment projects. But families are still living in many run-down buildings. People of all backgrounds, many of them Spanish-speaking, make their homes in this area.

American Jews now live in almost all the cities of the nation. There are 5.8 million Jews in the United States. This is only about 3 percent of the population, but it represents the largest Jewish community in the world. Over 2 million live in the

Greater New York area, with about 200 living as far north as Fairbanks, Alaska.

American Jews today work in all kinds of jobs, from taxi driver to college president. Most do skilled office or professional work because so many have high school and college educations. Over 90 percent of American Jewish youth enter college. As a result, the income for this group is high. But there are many poor Jewish families in the United States, too.

American Jews differ as much in looks as any other people. The color of their skin ranges from very fair to very dark.

No one has counted the exact number, but thousands of American Jews are black. These Jews live throughout the country. Some of them trace their heritage back to one of the original Hebrew tribes of Israel, and they call themselves Israelites. Black Jews are joining social groups, attending camps, and visiting Israel with their fellow American Jews.

These young Jews are members of Hatzaad Harishon, a Jewish social club. They perform folk dances.

Sammy Davis, Jr. the entertainer, is a black Jew, but he was not born a Jew. After studying the religion, he adopted it as his own.

Recent immigrants to the United States have included Jews from Cuba. Almost all of them left the island after Fidel Castro's Communist government came to power in 1956. About 6,000 of these Jews have settled in Florida. Each year a few thousand people from Israel come to the United States with the hope of becoming citizens.

The Hasidic Jews in America have come from Poland since World War II. This group can be recognized by their clothing.

Like their fathers, Hasidic boys wear long side locks and wide-brimmed hats.

They wear the long black coats and wide-brimmed black hats of the Polish gentlemen of long ago. The men grow long sidelocks and beards. The Hasidic Jews keep the kosher and Sabbath laws very strictly. They live together in close community groups in Brooklyn and Spring Valley, New York, and in other parts of the country.

Jews today vary widely in how they practice their religion. Some young people are more religious-minded than their parents were. Although they may have had little religious training as youngsters, they now take college courses in Judaism and attend services. Some Jews go to temple rarely. Others make the temple the center of their life.

A religious school is usually part of the temple's program. Classes are held one or more times a week. The youngsters learn to read Hebrew, study Jewish history, and celebrate the holidays together. In Conservative and Reform temples, students of fifteen or sixteen who have completed the course of study are confirmed in May or June at a special ceremony for the whole class.

Jewish organizations play a large part in American Jewish life. Groups like the Young Men's Hebrew Association (YMHA) have clubs for young and old. The Hillel Foundation has 260 chapters at colleges in the United States. Jewish students meet at Hillel to attend services, talk over ideas, or take courses in Judaism.

Jewish women may join many different clubs. Every temple has a sisterhood, whose members give their services to the temple. Hadassah is one of the best-known women's organiza-

Teamwork for tolerance: Catholic students visit Temple Sinai in Sharon, Massachusetts, to learn about Jewish customs.

tions. It was started in 1912 by Henrietta Szold, the daughter of a Baltimore rabbi. Through its many chapters, Hadassah raises money for hospitals and schools in Israel.

American Jews support their self-help organizations through yearly fund drives. They also have organizations which preserve Jewish thought and learning. One of these is Yivo Institute for Jewish Research in New York City. This institute has a library of Yiddish writings by European and American scholars. It gives courses in Yiddish so that modern men and women may understand their past.

Jewish-Americans take part in many interfaith activities. Temple youth groups exchange visits with church groups. The

National Conference of Christians and Jews works for cooperation among faiths.

Prejudice toward Jews still continues, but important advances have been made in recent years.

In 1969, the Catholic Church in Rome called for friendship and brotherhood between Christians and Jews. American Catholic bishops were quick to respond. They issued a statement that recalled the long persecution of Jews and said: "Christians ask pardon of their Jewish brothers." They worked out "guidelines for Catholic-Jewish relations" which present many ideas for cooperation. As a result, rabbis have been invited to give courses to teachers in Catholic schools in order to deepen their appreciation of Judaism.

Richard J. Schwartz, volunteer fund-drive chairman of the Federation of Jewish Philanthropies, visits a young patient at Blythedale Children's Hospital.

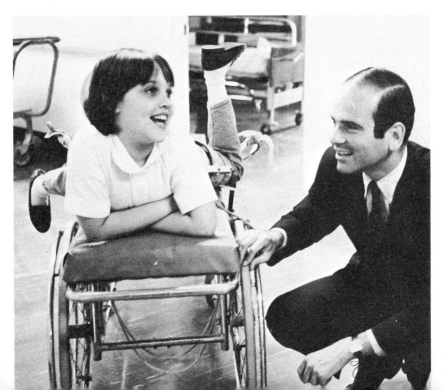

The United States has been built by many different groups who have been able to work together. The special qualities of each group contribute to the richness of American life. Jewish love of learning, self-help ideas, foods, and literature have become part of the American culture. The Jews in other lands and times were a people kept apart. In the United States, they share as equals in the growth of the nation.

Some Well-Known Jewish-Americans

Abramovitz, Max, Architect, 1908–

Aleichem, Sholom, author, 1859–1916

Baruch, Bernard, financier, 1870–1965

Bellow, Saul, author, 1915–

Benjamin, Judah P., U.S. senator, 1811–1884

Berlin, Irving, composer, 1888–

Bernstein, Leonard A., composer, 1918–

Brandeis, Louis, jurist, 1857–1941

Cahan, Abraham, author, publisher, 1860–1951

Cardozo, Benjamin N., jurist, 1870–1938

Celler, Emanuel, U.S. congressman, 1888–

Davis, Sammy Jr., entertainer, 1921–

Dubinsky, David, labor leader, 1892–

Einstein, Albert, physicist, 1879–1955

Epstein, Mike, baseball player, 1943–

Flexner, Simon, physician, 1863–1935

Fortas, Abraham, lawyer, 1910–

Frankfurter, Felix, jurist, 1882–1965

Gell-Mann, Murray, physicist, 1929–

Gershwin, George, composer, 1898–1937

Gimbel, Bernard F., philanthropist, 1885–1966

Goldberg, Arthur J., lawyer, 1908–

Goldberg, Bertram, architect, 1913–

Goldberger, Joseph, research scientist, 1874–1929

Gompers, Samuel, labor leader, 1850–1924

Greenberg, Hank, baseball player, 1911–

Greenberg, Jack, lawyer, 1924–

Guggenheim, Meyer, philanthropist, 1828–1905

Hackett, Buddy, entertainer, 1924–

Heifitz, Yasha, violinist, 1901–

Hellman, Lillian, playwright, 1907–

Hillman, Sidney, labor leader, 1887–1946

Hiltzik, Dean, skater, 1953–

Horowitz, Vladimir, pianist, 1904–

Jacobi, Abraham, physician, 1830–1919

Javits, Jacob, U.S. senator, 1904–

Kaye, Danny, entertainer, 1913–

Kallen, Horace M., philosopher, 1882–

King, Alan, entertainer, 1927–

Koufax, Sandy, baseball player, 1935–

Land, Edwin H., inventor, 1909–

Lasker, Albert, philanthropist, 1880–1952

Lazarus, Emma, poet, 1849–1887

Lefrak, Samuel, builder, 1918–

Lehman, Herbert H, governor, U.S. senator, 1878–1963

Leonard, Benny, boxer, 1896–1947

Levenson, Sam, entertainer, 1911–

Levy, Uriah, commodore U.S.N., 1792–1862

Lopez, Aaron, trader, 17? –1782

Malamud, Bernard, author, 1914–

Marshall, Louis, lawyer, 1856–1929
Menuhin, Yehudi, violinist, 1916–
Merrill, Robert, opera singer, 1919–
Michelson, Albert A., physicist, 1852–1931
Miller, Arthur, playwright, 1915–
Millstein, Nathan, violinist, 1904–
Morgenthau, Henry, Jr., cabinet member, 1891–1945
Ochs, Adolph S., publisher, 1858–1935
Oppenheimer, J. Robert, physicist, 1904–1967
Peerce, Jan, opera singer, 1904–
Rabi, Isador Isaac, physicist, 1898–
Ribicoff, Abraham, governor, U.S. senator, 1910–
Rickover, Hyman, admiral U.S.N., 1900–
Rose, Billy, impressario, 1899–1966
Rose, Ernestine, suffragette, 1810–1892
Rosenwald, Julius, philanthropist, 1862–1923
Ross, Barney, boxer, 1909–1967
Sabin, Albert, research scientist, 1906–
Salk, Jonas E., research scientist, 1914–
Salomon, Haym, philanthropist, 1740–1785
Salvador, Francis, patriot, 1748–1775

Sarasohn, Kasriel R., publisher, 1835–1905
Sarnoff, David, engineer, 1891–
Schick, Bela, research scientist, 1872–1967
Schiff, Jacob H., philanthropist, 1847–1920
Shamsky, Art, baseball player, 1941–
Shahn, Ben, artist, 1898–1969
Sills, Beverly, opera singer, 1929–
Singer, Isaac Bashevis, author, 1904–
Soyer, Moses and Raphael, artists, 1899–
Spitz, Mark, swimmer, 1950–
Spitz, Nancy, swimmer, 1954–
Stein, Gertrude, author, 1874–1946
Stern, Isaac, violinist, 1920–
Straus, Isidor, philanthropist, 1845–1912
Straus, Nathan, philanthropist, 1845–1912
Strauss, Levi, manufacturer, 1830–1902
Szold, Henrietta, philanthropist, 1860–1945
Touro, Judah, philanthropist, 1775–1854
Tucker, Richard, opera singer, 1915–
Waksman, Selman, biologist, 1880–

INDEX